Original title:
Into the Wildwoods

Copyright © 2025 Creative Arts Management OÜ
All rights reserved.

Author: Sebastian Whitmore
ISBN HARDBACK: 978-1-80567-165-7
ISBN PAPERBACK: 978-1-80567-464-1

The Dance of Whispering Pines

In the forest where trees sway,
A squirrel skips, leading the way.
With acorns tossed as they prance,
Even rabbits join the dance.

Mossy logs are their stage,
As frogs hop with great rage.
Woodpeckers drum and chime,
Turning nature into rhyme.

A bear rolls by, full of cheer,
While chipmunks giggle, 'Oh dear!'
The winds howl, but don't fret,
For laughter's the sweetest duet.

As night falls, the stars align,
A raccoon steals a birthday pine.
With shadows swirling, the fun begins,
Nature's party, where all friends win!

Secrets of the Leafy Canopy

High above where the branches twist,
The parrot chats, not to be missed.
Every leaf has a tale to tell,
Of mischief, laughter, and all's well.

A sloth hangs by, so very slow,
While below, ants march in a row.
They giggle at his lazy craze,
Waving like they're in a daze.

The owls hoot with a wise old spin,
"Who's having fun? Oh, let's dive in!"
The raccoons sneak some snacks at night,
Turning shadows into sheer delight.

With whispers of secrets under the sun,
In the leafy world, there's endless fun.
So tiptoe softly, join the spree,
In the canopy, wild as can be!

Trail of the Forgotten Souls

On paths where few dare to tread,
The ghosts of laughter still widespread.
Footsteps echo in silly tunes,
While owls hoot out of tune by moons.

A jester's hat on a tree limb hangs,
As foxes dance and the birdies sang.
The tales they tell of quirks and tricks,
Are worth more than a hundred gigs.

Fallen leaves whisper a jogger's tale,
Of mishaps and giggles that won't regale.
The spirits swap ghost stories bold,
While sneaky squirrels make off with gold.

So venture forth, if you are brave,
For in this trail, there's fun to save.
Where the forgotten souls still tease,
And play with mischief in the breeze!

Sunbeams through the Canopy

In the morning glow, the sunbeams peek,
The forest wakes up with a cheeky squeak.
Bunnies bounce in a golden light,
Chasing shadows with all their might.

Beams dance down to find a mouse,
Sipping dew inside a tiny house.
The sun, a joker on nature's clock,
Makes flowers giggle, tick-tock, tick-tock.

A cat naps lazy on a stone,
Dreaming of fish in a world of his own.
The light plays tricks with colors bright,
As butterflies twirl in sheer delight.

So join the sun's playful parade,
In the canopy, where joy is made.
With laughter sung from every part,
Nature's canvas is a work of heart!

Luminescence of the Forest Floor

Beneath the trees where shadows play,
The mushrooms dance in bright array.
A critter sneezes, what a sound,
As chuckles echo all around.

A squirrel juggles acorns wide,
While rabbits bounce in joyful stride.
The flowers giggle, petals toss,
As twirling vines make all of us.

The sunlight flickers through the leaves,
As nature's prankster tricks and weaves.
Gnarly roots form silly paths,
Where laughter sparks and never quaffs.

So come along, let's follow trails,
Where every twig and fern prevails.
In giggling woodland's merry spree,
We'll find the jest in harmony.

The Untamed Spirit of Woodlands

An owl hoots jokes from up high,
While chipmunks roll with laughter nigh.
A bear attempts a waltz so grand,
And trips upon a sleeping band.

The brook gurgles tales both bold,
Of dandelions brave and old.
The trees, they whisper silly puns,
As bushes chuckle 'neath the suns.

A raccoon, flaunting goggles bright,
Takes selfies with a flash at night.
The owlets wink, they know the score,
As laughter ripples evermore.

Where winds carry secrets, soft and sly,
A congregation of all who fly.
In the wilds where spirits play,
Life's goofy sketches lead the way.

Harmony of the Woodland Realm

In the thicket, mischief brews,
With sunny rays and quirky hues.
A fox in boots, a hat askew,
Prances on by, just for a view.

The birds rehearse their funny lines,
While laughter bursts in leafy shrines.
The pine trees sway in perfect cheer,
To melodies that all can hear.

A hedgehog runs a bustling shop,
With silly hats that make you hop.
The bartering critters find their way,
With jokes and jests that brighten day.

In this realm where laughter glows,
The harmony of fun just flows.
So dance along the woodland floor,
With giggles shared forevermore.

Journey through Mist and Moss

In a maze of mist, the paths unwind,
Where giggling critters seem to mind.
The mushrooms give a hearty cheer,
As wanderers pass and draw near.

The pines wear cloaks of morning dew,
With jesters frolicking, it's true!
A snail, with swagger, creeps along,
In sync with nature's silly song.

The mist giggles, whispering light,
As shadows join in sheer delight.
The mossy beds, a cozy nest,
Invite the weary for a jest.

So frolic forth, embrace the jig,
For woodland fun is oh so big!
With laughter woven in each step,
Our journey's where the wild is kept.

A Tapestry of Woodland Whispers

Squirrels plot a daring heist,
Acorns rolling, such a feast!
While laughing fawns take joyful leaps,
Around the trees, the mischief creeps.

A raccoon dons a fancy hat,
Claims he's royal—what of that?
Chasing butterflies, a hint of flair,
While owls wink with knowing stares.

The brook gurgles a silly song,
Fish dance beneath, they all belong.
The hedgehogs tumble, lose their way,
Roll around, then shout hooray!

Beneath the branches, shadows play,
In this quirky, wild ballet.
Nature's laughter fills the air,
A place where whimsy loves to dare.

The Language of the Living Glade

Bunnies gossip in hushed tones,
While frogs croak buzz like lively drones.
A parrot tells jokes, quite absurd,
As the woodland shakes with each word.

Mice fashion capes from fallen leaves,
Pretend they're knights, oh how it weaves!
A troupe of ants forms a parade,
Marching along, a silly charade.

The sunlight winks through tangled vines,
Crafting shadows like silly signs.
With whispers of mischief in the breeze,
The leaves chuckle, rustling with ease.

Caught mid-brouhaha, a deer can't hide,
With berries smeared on her side.
In a world where nonsense reigns supreme,
Life's a giggle, or so it seems.

Beneath the Soft Pine Hush

A chipmunk hoards with flair so proud,
While starlings form a gossip crowd.
They chirp about the day's best finds,
In whispered tones, such silly kinds.

The mushrooms wear their polka dots,
Raving about their funky spots.
A snail claims speed—what a dream,
Yet slides along at its own seam.

With whispers of the pine so sweet,
Squirrels dance to an offbeat beat.
Through cozy nooks and crannies tight,
They play hide and seek, what a sight!

Beneath the hush where stories blend,
The woodland creatures laugh, transcend.
With every rustle, giggles rise,
In this playful realm, no surprise.

The Enchantment of Overgrown Trails

With tangled paths where secrets hide,
A kerfuffle stirs as squirrels collide.
They launch acorns like little bombs,
And ducks quack out offbeat psalms.

The fox in shades dons a dapper tie,
Winks with mischief in his eye.
Jays cackle at the show of flair,
While vines twist whimsically in the air.

Bumbles bees buzz with a joke to tell,
As blossoms dance, casting a spell.
A hedgehog rolls with a puffed-up pride,
Claiming he's the queen of the wild glide.

With whispers alongside trail's embrace,
Laughter echoes through this space.
Nature's antics, a grand display,
In every nook, mirth leads the way.

Hidden Trails and Twilit Tales

A squirrel stole my sandwich, oh what a fuss,
He chattered and danced, a little nutty bus.
I chased him through brambles, slipped on some dew,
He grinned as he scattered my lunch in a queue.

Behind every bush, there's a new hidden jig,
Where raccoons wear masks and hold their own gig.
The trees start to chuckle, their branches a-shake,
As I trip on a root, face-down in a lake.

The owl hoots in laughter, while frogs cheer along,
A chorus of croaks joins my clumsy song.
I ponder at twilight, with mud on my face,
This wildwood adventure, a true comic race.

So if you seek wonder, just follow your nose,
And watch out for squirrels, they'll eat all your hose!
With giggles and twirls, the forest is grand,
Shared chuckles with critters, oh isn't it grand!

Caressing the Edge of the Wild

A hedgehog named Henry was quite the celebrity,
He danced on a log with such great agility.
He twirled and he spun, with a prickly appeal,
Wowed the woodland creatures, our own circus reel.

The deer tried to join, but tripped on a root,
And fell into flowers, what a sight, oh so cute!
A bear with a bow tie led the foxtrot alone,
While the rabbits brought snacks, oh what a fun zone!

Under the stars, they would laugh through the night,
With jokes and tall tales that brought pure delight.
The moon winked above, so eager to play,
As critters in costumes danced bright 'til the day.

So tiptoe the edges, where laughter is found,
In meadows of mischief, with joy all around.
At the edge of the wild, where silliness swells,
Embrace every giggle, and hear the woods' yells!

Petals on the Forest Breeze

Petals afloat like confetti in air,
A bee in a top hat, a buzz with great flair.
He tips his small brim, oh what a fine sight,
While flowers are bopping, they're all feeling light.

A snail with a shell, polka-dots in a row,
Raced a jaunty old turtle, what a quirky show!
But the race took a turn when they hit a big stone,
They slugged it out laughing, what a funny tone.

The breeze sang a tune, like a jester in play,
Whispering secrets, come dance, come sway!
The trees clapped their branches, all swaying in time,
To the rhythm of petals, a sweet silly rhyme.

So frolic in gardens where chaos can bloom,
Follow the giggles, let joy lift the gloom.
On the petals of laughter, let your spirit be free,
In the dance of the woods, you'll find glee, joy, and glee!

In the Arms of the Timeless Trees

The trees stood so tall, like grandpa in shade,
While whiskers of moss made his beard well displayed.
A raccoon in glasses gave him a wink,
"Take it easy, old timer, don't take life to stink!"

The branches were tickled by wind's playful tease,
As squirrels played hopscotch with such eager ease.
A hedgehog declared, "Let the games now begin!"
While owls rolled their eyes, tossing out silly grins.

In a silent debate, the flowers chimed in,
"Let's turn up the fun, let's all spin and spin!"
So they twirled in a circle, a colorful spree,
In the arms of those giants, what pure jubilee.

So come join the laughter, let your worries take flight,
In the woods where the timeless sing sweet through the night.
With each mossy giggle and sunlight that beams,
Embrace every moment, live wild with your dreams!

Surrender to the Woodland Mystique

In shadows deep where squirrels prance,
The rabbits hold a twirling dance.
Mushrooms giggle, trees do sway,
Join the fun, don't run away.

A raccoon dons a silly hat,
While busy bees chase after that.
The sunbeams tickle all around,
Where laughter is the only sound.

A breeze that whispers all the news,
Of joyous deer in muddy shoes.
A fox with flair struts down the lane,
It's all just one big woodland game.

So let your worries fall away,
Here in the woods, we laugh and play.
Surrender now to the delight,
For woodland cheer is purest bright.

The Silence Between the Trees

The trees are talking, can't you hear?
Whispers filled with woodland cheer.
A quirky owl blinks, looks bemused,
While chipmunks argue, quite confused.

The pines are stifling giggles low,
As beetles race in a wild show.
A woodpecker's got jokes to tell,
And every laugh echoes so well.

Caterpillars on a leaf parade,
In polka dots, they're grandly made.
No serious thoughts allowed today,
Just chuckles in this leafy bay.

So next time you find silence there,
Remember fun is everywhere.
In every rustle, see the jest,
In this green space, we are blessed.

Magic in the Twilight Glade

In twilight's glow, the fireflies dance,
Their little lights weave a silly trance.
The crickets laugh with a chirpy tune,
While frogs croak out a silly rune.

The moon peeks through like a curious friend,
As shadows stretch and twist and bend.
A raccoon winks with a twinkle bright,
Sharing secrets in the fading light.

The breezes carry giggles near,
As twigs and branches play sincere.
In this glade of laughter and fun,
The wild whispers of night begun.

So come and join this merry spree,
Where magic lives, as wild as can be.
In twilight's glow, we'll make our mark,
With humor bright against the dark.

The Nature of Dreaming Wild

In dreams of leaves and playful things,
The woodland hum with joy it brings.
The rabbits bounce on clouds of fluff,
And every creature says, "Enough!"

The owls spread tales of whimsical plight,
Where squirrels challenge stars at night.
A dance-off happens under the moon,
As even raccoons sing a tune.

The branches sway with glee as they hum,
To rippling laughter, all thoughts succumb.
In wildness found, we laugh and smile,
As nature shows the art of style.

So drift into this dreamlike scheme,
Where every moment's a silly theme.
Embrace the charm of twilight's yield,
In this land where joy is revealed.

Beneath the Boughs of Time

Beneath the boughs, a squirrel stands,
With acorns piled in both its hands.
It chases shadows, leaps, and bounds,
While giggling softly at silly sounds.

The wind whispers secrets, tickles the leaves,
The branches shake, a dance that deceives.
A fox struts by, wearing a hat,
Looking quite dapper, imagine that!

A raccoon joins, with bandit grace,
Stealing snacks from the picnic place.
They laugh and play without a care,
With nature's wonders everywhere.

Amidst the trees, a game unfolds,
Adventures in stories that never get old.
Time moves slowly, laughter flows,
In this woodland circus, anything goes.

The Wandering Spirit of the Ferns

Among the ferns, a spirit roams,
With sandals made of twigs and bones.
It hums a tune, a silly song,
While prancing along, where it belongs.

A woodpecker joins, with a hammer loud,
Trying to impress the gathering crowd.
The spirit chuckles, twirls around,
While beetles march on the grassy ground.

They hold a dance beneath the sky,
With laughter soaring, spirits high.
A frog in a bow tie croaks a beat,
Creating rhythms for tiny feet.

As dusk descends, the spirits play,
Underneath the stars that light the way.
Nature laughs in splendid tones,
In the heart of trees, they find their homes.

Essence of the Wild Pathways

On paths untamed, there's mischief afoot,
A rabbit in boots, looking quite cute.
It hops with flair, doing a jig,
While chasing after a wandering twig.

A tortoise frowns, with a steady pace,
As the rabbit zips, a hyper race.
"Slow down, dear friend," it says with glee,
"I'll win the day with strategy!"

Nearby, a chameleon makes a splash,
Changing colors, a vibrant flash.
"Look at me!" it grins, "A rainbow delight!"
As fireflies twinkle, lighting the night.

The pathways twist through joy and jest,
In nature's mirth, they find their rest.
Together they laugh, by moonlight's gleam,
In the essence of wild, they live the dream.

Tread Softly on Ancient Earth

Tread lightly, friends, where giants stand,
With roots like fingers in the land.
A bear in pajamas snoozes on high,
While dreaming of honey that's stacked to the sky.

A rabbit hops by, eyes wide with glee,
Trading wild tales with an old bumblebee.
They chat about mushrooms that dance in the night,
As the stars join the fun, twinkling bright.

In the underbrush, laughter is spun,
With quirky critters having their fun.
A parade of chipmunks, striped and proud,
Makes their way, like a bustling crowd.

So step with care on this ancient space,
Where nature's laughter fills every place.
With every step, a joyful sound,
In this lively theatre that we've found.

Shadows Dancing Among the Trees

In the shade of leafy hats,
Squirrels plot and dream of chats.
Mice hold a concert in the glade,
While frogs march to their serenade.

Beneath twinkling stars that wink,
Owls sip tea and start to think.
A rabbit dons a dapper tie,
Says, "Why not dance?" under the sky.

Twisted branches stretch and sway,
Hiding giggles from the fray.
Foxes try their hand at pranks,
Shadows join the merry ranks.

So if you wander near the grove,
Look for jests that twirl and rove.
In this place of jinks and fun,
Nature laughs with everyone!

Reverie of the Wandering Path

A path that winds like a clown's bow tie,
Hiccups of laughter as I pass by.
Each step is tickled by the breeze,
As I stumble over mismatched knees.

There's a mole wearing stylish shoes,
He winks and fills my head with views.
Each rock has stories it can tell,
Of apples stolen, and bats that fell.

The trees gossip like old pals,
While squirrels plan their wild hydrangeas.
The sun peeks through with a big smile,
"Let's act like goofballs for a while!"

I hop and skip on this carefree road,
Following whispers from the toad.
In this land of giggles and cheer,
I find the wild's delight right here!

Echoes of the Untamed Realm

An echo bounces, quite absurd,
A goat recites its favorite word.
Laughter rings, a melody,
As raccoons dance with jubilee.

Twirling leaves in a playful chase,
The winds join in this merry race.
Chickens strut with feathers bold,
While stories of silliness unfold.

The babbling brook tells quirky tales,
About owls dressed in floppy veils.
Every rustle and chirp in flight,
Adds to the wildwood's delight.

Nature's laughter on repeat,
Brings cheer to each wandering feet.
In this realm, we're all quite mad,
Where every creature's a little glad!

Beneath the Emerald Boughs

Beneath the boughs so emerald bright,
I spy a gopher with a kite.
It's tangled high in a leafy snare,
While chipmunks point and laugh in air.

A picnic planned for the ants that found,
Carrots and crumbs spread all around.
But oh no! A hungry bird in flight,
Turns the feast into a frightful sight!

A badger gloats over a giant cheese,
"Who knew wild life would be such a tease?"
With each chuckle, the forest bends,
In silliness, the day ascends.

So if you wander, take a peek,
For heaps of humor hide and sneak.
Among the trees, joy does abound,
In every giggle, life is found!

Resilience Amongst the Rustle

In the midst of leaves that sway,
A squirrel pondered on his way.
He tripped on acorns, felt quite clumsy,
Yet laughed it off, he's never grumpy.

A raccoon danced, a wobbly jig,
With every step, he took a big dig.
He stumbled twice on his own two feet,
Yet still declared, life is a treat!

Beneath the ferns, a gala unfolds,
With critters sharing stories bold.
The fox cracked jokes, the owl rolled eyes,
Together they made the forest rise.

Through laughter and leaps, friends intertwined,
In the wild, joy is what they find.
For every tumble, a giggle nearby,
In nature's heart, they'll always fly.

Portraits of the Hidden Glade

In a glade where shadows play tricks,
A rabbit painted with clownish flicks.
His brush, a twig, his palette, the ground,
With every stroke, joy would abound.

A chubby hedgehog snored by the brush,
Dreaming of snacks in a comical hush.
When he awoke with a frantic start,
He rolled away, a living art!

The deer pranced in polka-dotted cheer,
Wearing flowers as crowns, oh dear!
They twirled through daisies, free-spirited and bold,
Creating a spectacle, a sight to behold.

In the hidden glade, laughter resounds,
Echoing through all the joyous grounds.
With colors and quirks, they dance and sway,
In nature's gallery, where fun leads the way.

Whispers of the Ancient Grove

In the ancient grove, a secret scout,
A wise old owl began to shout.
"Have you heard the rumors?" he hooted with glee,
"The squirrels are planning a nutty spree!"

The underbrush shook with giggles and pings,
As chipmunks prepared to flaunt their bling.
With acorn hats and twiggy canes,
They marched in lines, through sun and rains.

A badger grinned, his whiskers a-fluff,
He sells all sorts of woodland stuff.
"A potion for giggles? Just five acorns!"
He winked and sold it, amidst the morns.

In whispers they spoke, with chuckles so light,
Frolicsome tales that dazzled the night.
In the ancient grove, joy takes its flight,
A parade of laughter, an endless delight!

The Secrets Beneath the Canopy

Beneath the canopy, rustles of mirth,
A caterpillar claimed he was best on the earth.
He tried to swagger, but tripped on a leaf,
Yet spun a yarn, oh what a belief!

The spiders wove webs, intricate and fine,
Yet one got stuck, feeling quite benign.
"I'm part of the show," she laughed in her plight,
A sticky situation that felt just right.

With mushrooms in hats and fireflies bright,
They gathered for potions, brewing delight.
A frog flipped a pancake, four feet in the air,
Landing with style, a perfect flair.

In this vibrant world, where wonders reside,
Laughter is magic, let joy be our guide.
For beneath every canopy, secrets unfurl,
A humorous dance in this whimsical whirl!

Serenity in the Forest's Heart

Amidst the trees, a squirrel leaps,
Chasing shadows, he never sleeps.
A crow caws loudly, sounding proud,
While pinecones tumble, drawing a crowd.

Frogs wear crowns of mossy green,
Bouncing jokes like kings, so keen.
Deer in pajamas, soft and bright,
Join a dance that lasts till night.

Tales Told by Twisting Vines

Vines gossip softly, twisting round,
Whispering secrets in leafy sound.
A raccoon sneaks, so sly and quick,
Swiping snacks like a furry trick!

Bears wear glasses, reading books,
Napping under the careful looks.
Squirrels attend a comedy show,
Filled with acorns and jokes to throw.

Sanctuary Beneath the Branches

Beneath the branches, a picnic waits,
While owls debate their dinner plates.
Bugs in bow ties, dance in pairs,
And chipmunks play tag without any cares.

Fiddling foxes serenade the stars,
As laughing thrushes strum guitars.
A wise old turtle takes a stroll,
With thoughts as deep as a wishing hole.

Flickering Lanterns in Verdant Shadows

Lanterns flicker in the night,
Fireflies twirl in dazzling flight.
A hedgehog juggles with great flair,
While rabbits giggle without a care.

In the moonlight, shadows prance,
Creatures leap and join the dance.
The tree trunks wear a festive grin,
Inviting all the fun to begin.

Tales of the Whispering Leaves

The leaves they chatter, oh so bright,
Telling secrets of squirrels at night.
A rabbit in glasses, reading a book,
By the old oaks, with a curious look.

The mushrooms dance, in a fancy ball,
With twirls and spins, they give it their all.
A raccoon in socks, taps his tiny feet,
Singing loud tunes, oh what a sweet treat.

Dancing shadows tease the glade,
As fireflies play, in their glimmering parade.
A wise old owl gives a bemused stare,
While raccoons kite-fly without any care.

What a ruckus! What a delight!
In the whispers of leaves, all feels just right.
Come join the laughter, oh take a chance,
In the twirling forest, where dreams prance.

A Sanctum of Stone and Root

Among the stones where the roots entwine,
A chipmunk dressed royal, sips on pine wine.
He sips and he spills, such a clumsy lad,
While the trees shake with laughter, and a bit sad.

A hedgehog in armor, declares a great feast,
Inviting all critters—both great and least.
But the ants bring a cake, quite massive indeed,
While the porcupine grins, this place is a need!

The echoes of giggles from cozy nooks,
As creatures exchange their favorite books.
A beaver in glasses, reads stories of yore,
Of mischief and laughter, and so much more.

Oh dear, what a mess, the scene has now sprawled,
With giggling and squeaking, they're having a ball.
The forest, it sways with playful delight,
In this sanctum of stone, where all feels just right.

The Light that Dares to Wander

A firefly flickers, with dreams on the run,
She dances on air, oh what ridiculous fun!
With a wink and a twist, she twirls through the night,
Leading all critters in a sparkling flight.

Toadstools getting tipsy, with laughter so bright,
While frogs don monocles, what a curious sight!
They preach of fine wines from a nearby stream,
In this luminous bash, all creatures will dream.

A shadowy hedgehog plans mischief in style,
With hats made of leaves, he tries to beguile.
While squirrels sip acorns from tiny teapots,
The comedic chaos, oh, it surely hits spots!

The moon, now giggling, joins in the spree,
It bathes the wild glade in shimmer and glee.
With a wink and a glow, they dance till the dawn,
In the light that wanders, we all get drawn.

Breath of the Wildwood Spirit

There's a breath in the air, somewhat snickering sly,
As brambles and branches decide to fly high.
A boisterous breeze plays tag with the leaves,
While all of the critters share giggles and heaves.

The spirit of chuckles tickles the ground,
As mushrooms sprout noses, not making a sound.
A beetle clad in stripes hosts a fancy parade,
With ants waving flags, in the sun's never-fade.

The giant old trees lean in to listen,
To the tales of the forest that always glisten.
Where daisies gossip, and daisies tease,
Hiding from sunlight while dancing with ease.

Oh, the chuckling echoes, come join in the cheer,
With whispers of mirth that all creatures can hear.
In the breath of this spirit, let laughter take wing,
For the joys of the wildwood, forever we sing.

When the Wildflowers Speak

When daisies gossip, do they giggle?
Buttercups are bold, but oh so wriggle!
Every petal whispers a sneaky joke,
While bees breakdance, causing quite a poke.

The roses roll their eyes at thorns,
While daisies laugh like a bunch of scorns.
Sunflowers wave, with heads held high,
Making sure that all can comply.

Lavenders scent the air with cheer,
Sage's humor is deliciously dear.
With every breeze, they tickle the air,
In this flowered realm, giggles do flare.

So if you wander where colors sprout,
Listen closely, there's laughter about!
For every bloom has a tale to tell,
In the garden of chuckles, you'll dwell.

The Fables of the Fern-Laden Ledge

On a ledge of ferns, where squirrels convene,
The stories they spun were simply obscene.
With acorns of wisdom, they argue and jest,
Claiming walnuts are better, or so they suggest.

A hedgehog rolled by, his prickle like gold,
Telling tales of adventures, both brazen and bold.
While frogs led the chorus with ribbits of glee,
Pledging never to join any wild jamboree.

The fables spoke loud through leaves in the breeze,
As critters all gathered, their chatter at ease.
With laughter abounding from each furry muse,
Even the owls couldn't help but refuse!

For sage advice came wrapped in great jest,
With winks and sly grins, it was quite the fest.
So lean in and listen, if you happen to tread,
Where fables of ferns spin tales in your head.

Journey to the Heart of the Green Realm

In a land where the foliage tickles your toes,
Adventures await where the wild river flows.
A raccoon in sunglasses, cool and profane,
Waves to the deer, both dancing in rain.

Mushrooms in clusters gossip like pals,
Trading secret recipes for wild berry gals.
The owls in their wisdom hoot tunes out loud,
While skunks fashion colognes, oh how they're proud!

The babbling brook spills tales of delight,
As frogs throw a party beneath the moonlight.
In this heart of green, laughter's the key,
Where every bush giggles and dances with glee.

So pack up your courage, your chuckle, your cheer,
Join in the frolic, there's fun to endear!
For in this great journey, it's humor we find,
Lost in the wild, the world's so kind.

Where the Wild Things Muse

Where the wild things ponder, in topsy turvy ways,
The mushrooms are wise in the most comical phase.
The trees take a chuckle with branches so wide,
While clouds rain down laughter; it's joy they provide.

Each critter convenes with a cackle and cheer,
With gossiping squirrels that draw ever near.
Raccoons play cards under starlit skies,
Challenging owls, who blink in surprise!

The wind carries whispers, so funny and light,
Of tales from the meadows, to share every night.
The grass sways in rhythm with giggles so spry,
As the sun casts its glow, and the shadows comply.

In this magical realm, nonsense takes flight,
Where the wild things muse, it's a laugh of delight.
So venture with glee, let your spirit unwind,
In the laughter-filled wood, peace is what you find.

Moonlight Overleaf and Moss

Beneath the moon, the shadows dance,
A raccoon dons my empty pants!
The owls hoot with a cheeky grin,
While fireflies twinkle—let's begin!

Sassafras leads on an evening spree,
I trip on roots, oh woe is me!
But laughter echoes through the night,
As critters join the comical flight.

Hares play hopscotch, chasing dreams,
While hedgehogs wear their finest seams.
The trees clap hands in rhythm sound,
In this circus of joy, I am bound.

As dawn arrives, my antics fade,
Yet memories linger—wild and unscathed.
With whispers shared under leafy zephyrs,
The woodland giggles, full of quirk and plethers.

Whispers of the Woodland Siren

A siren sings from branches high,
Her voice sways like a butterfly.
I follow tunes, my legs a twirl,
Oh dear, I'm caught in this leafy whirl!

Squirrels laugh and toss me nuts,
They form a band, but I'm the klutz!
With acorns flying, I must take cover,
The woodland concert is like no other.

The mossy floor becomes my stage,
With every step, I feel a rage.
For in this prankster's realm I dwell,
Where every tree has its own tale to tell.

Back to earth, the notes collide,
The giggles of nature now decide.
With every ounce of joy I glean,
I bow to all, chaotic and serene.

Colors of Solitude in the Woods

In hues of green, I seek a space,
But stumble on a squirrel's race!
With every tree, a hue so bright,
Yet laughter blooms in every sight.

The path is painted with my quirks,
As critters dance, I watch their jerks.
For solitude is far from grim,
When woodland friends are in the whim!

Caterpillars cha-cha on a leaf,
While I giggle, causing mischief and grief.
The colors swirl, in pure delight,
In this painted joy, I take flight.

With nature's brush I leave my trace,
A patchwork quilt of silly grace.
Colors of solitude, wild and free,
Dance in the woods, just wait for me!

Dreams Weave in Twisted Vines

In tangled dreams where vines entwine,
I find a treasure, a daisy, a sign!
But tripping over my own two feet,
Turns glorious walks into slapstick feats.

A rabbit juggles twigs with flair,
While I attempt a graceful air.
With every tumble, my laughter spills,
The woodland winks, oh what a thrill!

The brambles giggle, the branches sway,
As creatures frolic—come what may.
Nature's circus, a merry hive,
Where mischief reigns and dreams come alive.

So let the vines weave stories bright,
Of giggling hearts and pure delight.
In tangled dreams, forever free,
I dance with joys that can't be beat!

Flora's Gentle Embrace

In the meadow where flowers jest,
Bumblebees buzz, feeling their best.
Petals whisper secrets in the breeze,
While daisies dodge ants with giggles and tease.

A butterfly slips in a patch of mud,
With a flurry of wings, starts a flower flood.
Squirrels chuckle from limb to limb,
As they see the garden, nature's whim.

The sun sneezes bright, as clouds pull away,
Colorful blooms dance, in the light they sway.
Everyone's laughing, even the toad,
In Flora's embrace, they share the abode.

But owls roll their eyes at this vibrant show,
Saying, "We'd prefer a more mellow glow."
Yet laughter is loud, and the day brightens,
As each petal gives way to nature's lighten.

The Smell of Rain on Thicket

Raindrops tumble through leaves above,
Filling the air with a scent we love.
Mice in the bushes dance on their toes,
While frogs croak tunes, as the storm slows.

A woodpecker sings, lost in its quest,
And squirrels get drenched, while putting on jest.
Every puddle reflects the silly,
As creatures collide, all getting frilly.

With laughter and splashes, they frolic around,
Worms pop out, wiggling from the ground.
While raccoons jest, striking poses with flair,
Claiming victory over the wet with their hair.

The thicket is sticky, a comedy zone,
As each animal plays, all feeling at home.
So let them rain down, let the skies spill,
In this earthy circus, all joy is fulfilled.

Tales from the Roots Below

Down where the roots intertwine and spin,
There's a whole world where the stories begin.
Worms whisper loudly, sharing their tales,
About cheeky ants and their tiny scale fails.

A wise old snail spins yarns of delight,
Of mushroom debates that last through the night.
"Who's the best chef?" they argue with glee,
While spiders knit webs for all of the tea.

Trenches of dirt hold laughter and fun,
As moles play poker, under moon and sun.
They snicker and snort at the chaos above,
While dreaming of truffles, the ground gets a shove.

So gather round friends, in this underground show,
As roots weave their stories, where secrets do flow.
With each wriggle and giggle, let the tales bloom,
In the maze of the earth, there's always room.

Twilight's Silent Floral Ballet

As twilight descends, the flowers take flight,
In a ballet of colors, beneath soft moonlight.
Petals pirouette, they sway and they spin,
While shadows of insects quietly grin.

A daisy triplets, with claps of their leaves,
Gardenias gossip as the last light weaves.
Roses are blushing, showing their charms,
While violets twirl to the gentle night's balms.

Fireflies jive, lighting the scene,
As crickets provide a humorous mean.
They play the tunes for the flowers' sway,
In this silent ballet, they dance through the gray.

So join in the laughter, as night takes its hold,
With winks from the blooms, and stories retold.
In the laughter of petals and soft evening dew,
Twilight's ballet reminds us of what's true.

Whispers of the Untamed Grove

Beneath the boughs, a squirrel pranks,
Dodging arrows from my flanks.
A raccoon steals my sandwich rare,
While I just stand and glare.

A bear in shades sips honey tea,
He offers me a taste, oh me!
I take a sip, it tastes like grass,
Now I'm not sure I want to pass.

The trees, they whisper secret jokes,
As owls roll eyes and giggle strokes.
I stumble through the tangled weeds,
Chasing after laughing seeds.

And though these woods can be a rout,
With all its cheers, I can't pull out.
For in this place of quirky sights,
Who wouldn't stay for silly nights?

Secrets Beneath the Canopy

The mossy floor suggests a dance,
But all I do is slide and prance.
A chipmunk winks with mischief bold,
And starts a round of tales retold.

In shadows deep, a frog will croak,
Telling jokes from an ancient yoke.
The bugs join in, a buzzing band,
Each one with humor tightly planned.

Thought I was wise, with careful tread,
Till I sat down on the wrong bed.
A patch of mushrooms—oh what fun!
Turns out they're for the lap of sun.

So secrets hide beneath green veils,
Where laughter echoes, whimsy sails.
In this light-hearted, leafy maze,
I learn to dance with silly praise.

Shadows Among the Ancient Pines

In shadows cool, a fox does strut,
With a swagger that's just a nut.
He tips his hat, adjusts his tie,
Then eats my snack without a sigh.

The pines, they mutter jokes so grand,
As I trip over a root so bland.
A raccoon laughs from a lowly branch,
While I do my best to prance.

I bump into a wise old tree,
It giggles, saying, "Come drink with me!"
I sip the sap, it tastes like wine,
Now I'm a fan of dining fine!

With chuckles shared in nature's den,
I find my joy time and again.
For every stumble, every fall,
Brings laughter to this wild, odd hall.

The Song of Forgotten Paths

Along the trail, a tune we find,
It's sung by roots, so intertwined.
The twigs can joke, and leaves can play,
As daylight dances, bright and gay.

A hedgehog mocks my muddy shoes,
While squirrels chat and share the news.
They gossip softly, share their thrills,
And laugh at all my clumsy spills.

The flowers giggle in their beds,
As bees buzz lightly over heads.
With laughter woven in each thread,
I join the song, just using my head.

In these wild paths, where fun abounds,
Nature's humor knows no bounds.
So let us all, with notes so clear,
Sing out our joy, and dare not fear.

The Lure of the Hidden Meadow

In a meadow not so far,
Bunnies dance beneath the star.
They wear hats, quite the sight,
Chasing fireflies in delight.

Old owls hoot a merrily tune,
While squirrels plot to steal a prune.
The grass tickles their tiny feet,
As they shimmy and sway to the beat.

A raccoon tries its luck at hide,
But forgets that trunks need good pride.
With branches stuck like a bad hairdo,
He blinks twice, what's a poor guy to do?

In this funny, silly glen,
The woodland plays a game again.
They laugh, they jiggle, they spin around,
In their hidden meadow, joy is found.

Constellations of the Sylvan Sky

Above the trees where owls complain,
Stars gossip, both friendly and plain.
One says, 'I could be a bear!',
But another boasts, 'Not with that hair!'

The raccoons ponder their bright fate,
As they think stars change their weight.
'If we're fluffy, we'll drift high!',
But one giggles, 'We'll just cry!'

Lightning bugs join the celestial brawl,
They flash and wiggle, trying to enthrall.
One blinks an idea, 'Let's form a band!',
And soon they all dance hand in hand.

So when you look up at night's great plume,
Remember the laughter of fluff and zoom.
In this sky, where creatures play,
The constellations giggle the night away.

Guardians of the Woodland Realm

In shadows deep where guardians roam,
A bear claims, 'This is my home!'
While chipmunks nod in sheer delight,
'Let's have a dance-off every night!'

The wise old fox has wisdom to share,
'If we prance, no one will care!'
With a twirl and a leap, they take flight,
In this realm, the mood is quite bright.

Deer in tutus leap with a glide,
The forest floor turns to a slide.
They topple over in a heap,
While giggles echo, oh so deep!

In the woodland, joy is the rule,
Where critters gather for their school.
Together they teach, they laugh, they play,
Guardians of fun in their own way.

Reflections in a Shimmering Stream

In a stream that sparkles with laughs,
Fish wear glasses as they do math.
They count the bubbles, one by one,
Chasing their tails, oh what fun!

Turtles sail on lilypad rafts,
Trading tales of their greatest gaffes.
While frogs croak 'Ribbit, you're bold!',
With giggles shared, the laughter's gold.

A beaver hums a silly song,
While the watermelons roll along.
They splash and dive, creating waves,
In this stream, happiness saves.

So skip a stone and give a cheer,
In this glowing stream, joy is near.
Reflection of laughter shines so bright,
In every ripple, pure delight.

Leaf and Lure

In the trees where squirrels leap,
Mushrooms dance and shadows creep.
A leaf fell down, it made a sound,
A critter jumped, he thought he drowned.

A buzzing bee, wearing a hat,
Found a peach that looked like a cat.
It rolled away, the bee in chase,
Now who's the funny one in this race?

A frog hopped by, with jester's flair,
Stole the bee's hat, light as air.
He croaked a tune, a silly jig,
While bugs gathered round for the gig.

Now every day, they laugh and play,
In the woods where mischief finds a way.
So join the fun, give it a whirl,
In this leafy world, let laughter swirl.

The Heartbeat of the Forest Floor

Beneath the trees, a heartbeat thumps,
It's just a bear, who's found some stumps.
He sat right down, to munch some ants,
And danced around in his silly pants.

A rabbit watched, with eyes so wide,
As the bear danced, he nearly cried.
"Come join me friend!" the bear did shout,
But all the rabbit thought was, "Get out!"

A raccoon joined, with shiny treats,
He brought along some old, mismatched beats.
They formed a band, with pots and pans,
And made a noise that resembled bands.

So if you wander where the woods play tunes,
Beware of bears and their funky moves.
For in the forest, fun won't cease,
A heartbeat booming, laughter's peace.

Fable of the Forgotten Glade

In a glade where the sun wouldn't shine,
There sat a toad, looking quite divine.
He wore a crown made of wilted leaves,
And sang of things that no one believes.

A snail crawled by with a swagger so bold,
Claiming his shell was made of gold.
"Oh please!" scoffed the toad, with a grin,
"Your gold is just dirt, now let's begin!"

The two then planned a grand parade,
To showcase all the woodland's brigade.
With critters prancing and laughter loud,
In the glade, they formed a silly crowd.

So if you find this glade of mirth,
With tales of jest and joyful birth,
Just remember, it's the friends you make,
That turn the forest into a giggle quake.

A Journey through Nature's Canvas

A painter tried to catch the sun,
But tripped on roots, oh what fun!
His easel fell, the colors flew,
And splattered on the chipmunk too.

"Now look at me!" the chipmunk squeaked,
"I'm a masterpiece!" he proudly peeked.
The painter laughed, "What a sight!"
With colors bright, they danced in delight.

A deer walked by with paint on her nose,
Wondering, "Is this how art grows?"
She joined the fun, with a swish of her tail,
Together they set off on a colorful trail.

So grab your brush, or just your cheer,
For every journey brings joy near.
In nature's canvas, don't just stand,
Join the wild fun, lend a hand!

Harmony of Fern and Fern

Ferns whisper secrets, they wiggle and dance,
In a playful rhythm, they take their chance.
A leaf tickles a toe, a breeze makes it sway,
Nature's party begins, it's a ferny ballet.

Mushrooms wear hats, the squirrels look on,
As crickets play fiddles from dusk until dawn.
With laughter so light that the branches all jiggle,
Even the shadows can't help but giggle.

A deer tries the cha-cha, but stumbles in glee,
While owls hoot laughs from their perch on a tree.
Petals throw confetti, the sky turns to glee,
Harmony echoes through each mighty spree.

Secrets Cradled in Earth and Sky

Beneath the old boughs where the wild things prance,
Lie whispers of history spinning in chance.
A mole tells a tale in a tunnel so wide,
While ants form a chorus, with giggles beside.

The clouds catch the chatter from the ground to the stars,
As flowers play poker with roots and guitars.
A squirrel cracks jokes from the top of a stump,
Adding comedy gold to a well-hidden hump.

The sun winks down, the moon starts to snicker,
As shadows do jiggles and sunlight grows thicker.
Secrets spin wildly, in the breeze they fly,
Cradled by laughter that never says bye.

A Lullaby for the Ancient Briar

Let's sing a soft tune to the old briar vine,
Who's tangled in stories, we sip herbal wine.
With thorns like snaggletooths, it guards all its dreams,
While birds chirp a chorus, or so it seems.

A butterfly winks like a crafty old sage,
As daisies roll eyes at the wise mossy page.
The briar hums softly, a bedtime delight,
With giggling fireflies flickering bright.

The moon croons a melody soft and so sweet,
As the briar sways gently to nature's own beat.
Its tangled embrace, where the wild things may roam,
Is a lullaby haven, forever a home.

In Search of Nature's Heart

With compass in hand and a map made of leaves,
We wander through giggles, where nature believes.
A hedgehog in spectacles leads us along,
Singing sweet sonnets where all creatures throng.

The breeze tells us tales of a mischievous owl,
Who hoots out the punchlines and makes the day howl.
The stream chuckles softly, a ticklish embrace,
While rocks crack a smile at our curious pace.

Every rustle and shuffle offers clues on the way,
As grasshoppers join in and start the ballet.
With mischief and laughter, we twist and we turn,
In search of that heartbeat for which we all yearn.

The Mystique of Moss-Covered Stones

Mossy rocks hold secrets tight,
Whispers of critters in the night.
I tiptoe softly, what do I find?
A frog in a crown, truly unkind!

The stones are squishy, a bouncy affair,
I jump and trip with a clumsy flair.
They laugh as I tumble, oh what a sight!
Nature's own jester, lost in delight.

In the Embrace of Nature's Breath

Leaves chuckle lightly in the soft breeze,
A squirrel throws acorns with utmost ease.
I dodge and I duck, my hat takes a flight,
Nature's own game of catch, oh what a plight!

Trees whisper jokes, ancient and wise,
Bark biting back with mischievous lies.
I grin at the chaos, a whirlwind of fun,
In this crazy theater, we dance as one.

The Call of the Untouched Thicket

In thickets so dense, I hear them sing,
A chorus of crickets, what joy they bring.
But wait, what's that? A twig snaps in jest,
A rabbit hops past, now that's quite a quest!

Lost in the thorns, with giggles abound,
I trip over roots, stuck in the ground.
But the laughter of bushes makes me forget,
In these wild corners, I'll never regret.

Reverie of the Hidden Glen

In a glen where shadows play peek-a-boo,
I spot a raccoon, oh what will he do?
With a burger in paws, he's king of the glen,
I watch in surprise, then giggle again!

Grass tickles my toes, as I roll and I spin,
The flowers are giggling, let the fun begin.
Nature's grand party, no invitation needed,
In this land of laughter, I'm joyfully greeted.

Echoes in the Underbrush

A squirrel named Nutty wore a bright hat,
He danced on the branches, a jolly chap.
The birds all laughed, flapping with glee,
While Nutty just grinned, as proud as can be.

A bear told a joke that was really quite bad,
His friends rolled their eyes, all feeling so sad.
But then came a rabbit, quick-witted and sly,
And they all burst out laughing, oh me oh my!

A raccoon with a knack for baking good pies,
Served them to friends, much to their surprise.
They feasted on treats, oh what a delight,
But left the poor raccoon alone for the night.

The trees whispered tales to the soft, breezy air,
While critters played tricks, with nibbles to share.
In the shade of the leaves, life's antics unfold,
A comedy show in the green, bright and bold.

Nestled in Nature's Cradle

A hedgehog in slippers rolled down the lane,
With acorn umbrella, he'd dance in the rain.
The frogs serenaded him, croaking a tune,
While fireflies twinkled like stars in the noon.

A wise old owl perched high on a pine,
Said, "Life's a big party, just sip on the brine!"
The raccoons chimed in, with a mischievous grin,
"Let's turn up the fun! Where do we begin?"

Then came a parade of skunks, singing loud,
With a funky old beat, they drew quite a crowd.
The deer, they all pranced, quite fancy and proud,
Waving to everyone, including the cloud.

As sunset descended, they shared a great laugh,
With shadows and giggles, they'd dance on the path.
In nature's embrace, where the wild critters play,
They cherished each moment, all night and all day.

Stories from the Bark and Stone

On a log sat a turtle, slow but oh so wise,
With stories of yore and twinkling green eyes.
A chatty old mouse piped up with a squeak,
"Tell us the tale of that brave little peak!"

He spoke of a rock that was known to declare,
"I'm tougher than diamonds! Just touch me, I dare!"
But no one believed it, they snickered and teased,
Until a chipmunk hopped, and the brave stone sneezed!

The laughter erupted, it echoed so sweet,
Even frogs stopped their croaking to join in the beat.
The stone felt so proud, he puffed up his chest,
"Look at me now, I'm a comedy fest!"

As the moon rose above, they chuckled and cheered,
A night full of giggles, so wild and so weird.
The bark and the stone, both part of the fun,
Creating memories 'til the day was all done.

Breath of the Forest Wind

The wind played a tune, like a playful flute,
It tickled the leaves, and danced with a root.
A fox with a scarf ran to join the parade,
While frogs jumped in rhythm, unafraid to cascade.

Mice in their sneakers raced around in delight,
Chasing after shadows that leaped in the light.
The owls hooted softly, adding to the glee,
"Who needs a dance floor? Just look at the trees!"

The flowers chimed in with their bright, spry tunes,
Brought life to the night, like colorful balloons.
And every little critter joined in with a cheer,
As the forest embraced the joy of the year.

With laughter a plenty, they twirled and they spun,
In the sweet gentle breeze, every creature had fun.
Nature's own comedy, played under the moon,
In the breath of the wind, their hearts sang in tune.

Chronicles of the Ancient Grove

In a forest thick with trees,
Squirrels wear their winter fleas.
They chatter loud, they flip and flop,
While old owls snooze and softly plop.

Mice dance in the dappled light,
Wearing acorn caps for their delight.
Rabbits hop in silly rows,
While bears attempt to do the toes!

A raccoon with a pie in hand,
Claims it's his "favorite brand."
He shares some crumbs, but what a mess,
The cleaning crew will say "no stress!"

And thus the tales of laughter spread,
With every creature's joy and dread.
For life in groves is pure delight,
When mischief stirs from day to night.

The Voice of the Wildflowers

Beneath the sun, the flowers argue,
"Look at me! I'm bright and true!"
Daisies giggle, roses blush,
While violets start to form a hush.

Tulips boast of height and flair,
Sunflowers say they're rarest rare.
But dandelions just laugh aloud,
"We're the ones that make you proud!"

Bees buzz in with silly grins,
"Who's the fairest? Let's begin!"
Over petals they do dance,
Planting seeds of pure romance.

And when the breezes gently sigh,
The blooms all wink and roll their eyes.
For in this field of colors bright,
There's joy and laughter at their height.

Dawn's Embrace in Hallowed Woods

When morning breaks on leafy greens,
The critters wake from wacky dreams.
A fox complains, "Where's my shoe?"
While raccoons munch on stolen stew.

A turtle speeds, oh what a sight,
Slow and steady wins it right!
While birds sing songs of silly tunes,
The sun peeks high, far past the moons.

A deer arrives with breakfast tray,
Spills the juice; what a display!
The squirrels laugh, they tip their hats,
"Watch out for those stray acrobat bats!"

As shadows stretch and dances start,
All creatures join with cheerful heart.
For dawn has come to jolly cheer,
Where laughter thrives, and skies are clear.

Chasing Shadows Beneath the Arching Boughs

Under branches, shadows play,
Chasing giggles all the way.
"Catch me!" calls a frolicking hare,
While squirrels just pretend to care.

A porcupine rolls down the hill,
Brushing off the snickers, "Chill!"
With every bounce, he squeaks and flops,
A sight that makes the laughter stop!

In puddles, puddles, splashes fly,
As frogs leap up, they touch the sky.
"Hold on tight! I'm not your friend,"
The wise old turtle cries, "Don't bend!"

So here they play from morn to night,
Cracking jokes in dimmest light.
For in these woods, the fun won't cease,
Chasing shadows, laughter's peace.

Cerulean Skies Over Emerald Keep

Squirrels in hats play chess on a log,
Beneath clouds shaped like a big, fluffy dog.
Birds tweet gossip about the mallard's new shoes,
While chipmunks debate the latest tree news.

One frog does the tango on a rock made of cheese,
While ants throw a party, dancing with ease.
The sun winks down with a glimmering grin,
As owls serve punch from a cup made of tin.

A turtle in flip-flops strolls by with a song,
Chasing butterflies who think they belong.
All creatures join in for the wildest parade,
Beneath those bright skies, a new game is played.

The Dance of Dusty Butterflies

Butterflies twirl in a flowery ballet,
Chasing each other the funnest way.
One wears a crown made of dandelion fluff,
The others all giggle, saying, "That's enough!"

A ladybug DJ spins tracks made of dew,
While crickets provide the best nighttime view.
Moths crash the party, feeling quite bold,
But they're just a bit too fuzzy and old.

They swap out their wings for a colorful veil,
And soon join the chorus, singing a tale.
With laughter and light, under soft, moonlit beams,
They dance through the night, chasing their dreams.

Rustling Leaves and Hidden Dreams

Leaves giggle as the wind whispers by,
Tickling the branches, oh my, oh my!
A fox wears bow ties, pretending to be chic,
While rabbits debate which carrot to tweak.

The bees hold a meeting to discuss honey,
While ants play charades, oh isn't that funny?
A stray beetle claims he's the king of the show,
But his royal scepter is just a dry leaf, you know!

With rustles and chuckles among the tall trees,
The forest provides a soundtrack to tease.
Each creature a player, each moment a scheme,
In the grand game of life, we all chase a dream.

A Journey Through Whispering Branches

Beneath the arching limbs, oh what a sight,
A moose learns ballet, thinking he's light.
While raccoons on stilts showcase their flair,
The laughter rings loudly, filled with fresh air.

A parrot sings opera, high in a tree,
While frogs juggle flies, drinking mint tea.
The squirrels cheer on, as acorns take flight,
In this world of wonder, all feels just right.

The shadows grow long, but spirits stay bright,
As critters share stories, their hearts full of light.
With giggles and joy, they embrace the night,
In a whimsical world, everything feels right.

Embrace of the Enchanted Thicket

In the brush, a squirrel prances,
Chasing shadows, taking chances.
A raccoon giggles, what a sight,
Stealing berries under moonlight.

A wise old owl raises his brow,
"Who put the berries here, and how?"
The fox just shrugs, twirls his tail,
"Just follow the fun; you can't fail!"

The trees shake hands with the breeze,
Whispers float like secret keys.
A porcupine rolls down a hill,
Laughs echo, oh what a thrill!

In this realm of playful grace,
Nature's jesters find their place.
With every step, a giggle sweet,
Come join the dance, feel the beat!

The Call of the Untrodden Trails

A turtle races, slow but proud,
"Catch me if you can!" he vowed.
The snails remarked, with laughter free,
"We're winning gold! Just wait and see!"

A chipmunk pauses, strikes a pose,
"Is my fur stylish? How it glows!"
As butterflies float, they twirl with flair,
While flowers giggle, scents fill the air.

Worms talk gossip beneath the ground,
"Did you hear what's happening around?"
The daisies blush at the juicy tale,
As nature whispers without fail.

Each trail tickles feet with glee,
Adventures bloom in wild decree.
Let's wander free, keen eyes aglow,
Follow the fun wherever it goes!

Sylvan Serenade at Dusk

As the sun dips low, shadows play,
The crickets begin their nightly sway.
A wise old toad croaks a tune,
While fireflies flash like tiny moons.

A band of raccoons set the scene,
With tambourines made of bright green.
They sing of stars that jump and tumble,
While nearby owls hoot and mumble.

The trees sway gently to their beat,
Offering branches for all to meet.
"Join our jam!" the bushes cheer,
As laughter echoes, drawing near.

When twilight wraps its cozy shawl,
The woodland creatures heed the call.
With hearts so light, they dance and sway,
In this serenade at close of day.

Mysteries Wrapped in Green

A little elf peeks from a leaf,
Hiding giggles, oh what a thief!
He nudges ferns, a silent trick,
"Try to catch me!" he snaps, then flicks!

Mossy stones hold secrets old,
Whispers of stories waiting to be told.
A hedgehog chuckles, rolling wide,
"Let's turn this forest into a slide!"

With sunlight dappling through the trees,
The laughter carries on the breeze.
A crow caws out, "What's the fuss?"
"Just fun!" they shout, as they all rush!

In this wild place, mysteries stir,
With every rustle, every purr.
Nature's laughter fills the night,
Wrapped in green, pure delight!

Underneath the Verdant Veil

Beneath the leaves where squirrels play,
A hedgehog dances, come what may.
With tiny shoes and fancy flair,
He spins around without a care.

The owls hoot jokes, a wise old crew,
While raccoons plan their heist for stew.
A rabbit laughs, he's lost his way,
His map was just a leaf today.

The mossy ground is soft and sweet,
Where mushroom hats are all the heat.
A critter's feast of berry pie,
Who knew that ants could dance and fly?

And here we sit, our hearts alive,
With giggles, gaffes, and silly jive.
The wild is full of quirky cheer,
So pull a chair, the fun is near!

Echoes of the Wilderness Heart

A chorus sung by crows at dawn,
They caw, they tease, they prance on lawn.
A deer in tights, a sight to see,
As he indulges in a spree.

Through trees adorned with giggling leaves,
The frogs croak rhymes, the beauty cleaves.
While crickets holler in the night,
Impromptu shows, such pure delight.

Around the brook, the minnows dart,
Play tag with fish, a lively art.
A turtle slowly joins the fray,
Says, "I'm just here to savor play!"

With every rustle, there's a cheer,
In nature's ring, there's no doubt here.
The wild sings songs of mirth and fun,
For laughter makes a day well spun!

The Lure of Untrodden Trails

In paths untamed, the stories weave,
A bear on wheels, who could believe?
He rolls along on tiny skates,
And jokes with squirrels about their plates.

The whispers dance among the trees,
Where bunnies boogie with such ease.
A raccoon chef, he flips the flap,
Creating meals from waste and scrap.

The fawns play tag with shooting stars,
While fireflies shine like neon cars.
A wise old tortoise holds the crown,
He's seen it all, yet never frown.

The trails invite with laughter strong,
Where nature's joys will hum a song.
So step right up, don't be so shy,
In this wild world, we soar and fly!

Sunlight Through Leafy Fingers

The sun peeks through with golden beams,
A dancing light that plays with dreams.
Where shadows stretch like silly grins,
The forest chuckles, and the fun begins.

With butterflies in wacky hats,
They fling confetti with the bats.
A game of hide and seek ensues,
For 'neath the blooms, they cannot lose!

The chipmunks wager on the breeze,
While nature's jokes still bring us ease.
A silly breeze, it grabs the leaves,
And whispers tales that everyone believes.

And as we laugh beneath the skies,
The wildwood twinkles with surprise.
With sunlight filtering through the trees,
It's laugh and live, our hearts at ease!

www.ingramcontent.com/pod-product-compliance
Lightning Source LLC
Chambersburg PA
CBHW051630160426
43209CB00004B/583